Contents

Stanley the Fierce

Stanley the Fierce
Has a chipped front tooth
And clumps of spiky hair.
And his hands are curled into two fat fists
And his arms are bulgy and bare.
And his smile is a tight little mean little smile
And his eyes give a shivery glare.
And I hear that he goes for seventeen days
Without changing his underwear.

But I don't think I'll ask him.

Judith Viorst

Spot the Difference

The two pictures look very much alike.
In both a boy is diving into a swimming pool.
A girl sits, dangling her feet in the water.
A nice woman in a flowery frock
Is pointing at something we cannot see.
And a faithful dog I have nicknamed 'Soldier'
Is standing guard over a tennis ball.
There is a table laid for a picnic tea.

I am spotting the differences. There should be ten.
Look. There's no logo on the second boy's trunks,
And the second girl has only one hair ribbon.
And mummy number two – her watch has gone.
I don't like it. The bird has flown from the sky,
There's an extra cloud on the horizon,
And the swimming pool ladder has lost some rungs.
(That's six.) Oh, and Soldier has only one eye.

Who has done this to these nice people?
Look. They've got no milk for their tea;
Their jug has disappeared. Somebody hates them –
There are only three legs to their picnic table.
Which leaves me with just one to get.
(And to think I thought both pictures the same!)
Got it! Where mummy is pointing – there in
  the shrubbery –
Among those badly drawn leaves, isn't that

The muzzle of a rifle? And who is it pointing at?

Gerard Benson

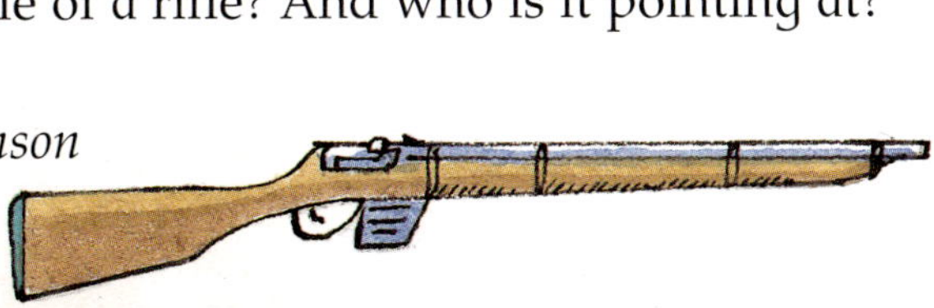

Spinning Homework

The spider with clumsy writing
Gets all the homework wrong
Pages tear with each spinning
And the words are very long.
He's bright at counting flies
Building webs up to the skies
Close to the sunrise.
With feet of eight
He's never late,
But the words are always jumbled
Homework book crumpled.
Sometimes numbers spin and shake
Pencils bend and break!
Sometimes he makes a sign
With books hanging on a line.

Faustin Charles

Hail Me!

Suddenly I came –
little ice bullets
instead of rain

I ping-ponged
on the rooftops
I spin-spun
in the gutters
I bounced down
on the concrete
I hit upon
the flowers
I rolled off
the edges
of window-ledges
and hedges

I lay around
for as long as I could
(which in my case was
only five minutes)
then I vanished.

Grace Nichols

Ode to Weight Lifting

Tony eats apples
On Saturday morning,
Two for each arm,
And one for the backs
Of his calves.
He's twelve
And a weight lifter in his garage.
He bites into an apple,
And, chewing,
He curls weights –
One, two, three…
His face reddens,
And a blue vein
Deepens on his neck –
Four, five, six…
Sweat inches down
His cheek. A curl of
Hair falls in his face –
Seven, eight, nine…
He grunts and strains –
Ten, eleven, twelve!
Tony curls his age,
And he would curl his weight
Of 83 pounds, but he
Would pull a muscle
In his arm.
Tony pulls off his T-shirt.
He flexes his biceps,
And apples show up in his arms.
"Pretty good," he says,
His fists clenched.
He takes another
Bite of apple,
And out of happiness
Bites the apples
In his biceps, tenderly
Of course. The teeth
Marks are pink,
His arms brown,
And his roar red as a lion's
With a paw swiping at air.

Gary Soto

Winter Haiku

Policemen pour out
of a riot van's siren
chasing the silence.

Helen Dunmore

Lorries Behind

The teeth of lorries in the driving mirror
the breath of lorries on the rear window

the hiss of lorries waiting to shoulder by,
the throb of diesel, the air-brake sigh

the hot shimmer in the driving mirror.
Lorries behind. Too close. *Look at that smile.*

Helen Dunmore

Round and Round

The handle swings the mallet
The mallet drives the wedge
The wedge cracks the tree trunk
With its cutting edge
The chainsaw comes roaring in to fell it
Then a carpenter takes a slice of the tree
And carves out the handle for a mallet

Adrian Mitchell

Eclipse of the Sun

I say the sun is a ball of hot gas
at the centre of the solar system.

You say it is the sky-god
in the centre of your life.

I say the sun is largely composed
of the elements hydrogen and helium.

You say its sacred substance
is fire which breathes life.

I say the sun is 150 million
kilometres distant from the earth.

You say it is where it is,
the heart of all things.

I say the sun burns at 6 thousand
degrees centigrade on its surface
and over 10 million at its centre.

You say kneel before it:
to stare directly at a god
will burn out your eyes.

I say the sun's gravitational field
is 28 times greater than the earth's.

You say the sun's power
enables you to walk upright
through your earth journey.

I say the sun emits light, X-rays,
radio waves, gamma and cosmic rays.

You say it wakens the earth
and enlightens the spirit.

I say the sun has a corona from which
electrically charged particles stream
into space forming vast solar winds
which affect the earth's weather.

You say the sun's bright halo
surrounds a god of great mercy
and from it stream all gifts.

I say the sun has spots and flares,
which vary both in size and number
if observed over a period of years.

You say your sky-god's face
expresses a great many moods.

I say the sun has supplied the earth
with light and heat energy for about
5 thousand million years and will
continue doing this for at least
another 5 thousand million years.

You say your shining is a brief
spark of the sun's eternity.

I say the sun is getting hotter:
in 5 thousand million years' time
it will become a giant star and life
on earth will probably be destroyed.

You say life on this earth
is a fragile thing: if it is
here tomorrow you will kneel
and thank the sky-god.

I say the sun has addled your brain
and therefore I must blindfold you.

You say the sun has let you
see your truth and it also
has let me see my truth.

I say that I must tie you to a pole
so you may denounce your beliefs.

You say that though the gun
may send fire to your head,
it cannot kill the sky-god.

I say the sun is a ball of hot gas
at the centre of the solar system.

You say nothing.

Norman Silver

The Sun Witness

Long ago a young girl
wearing a saffron coloured saree
walked gracefully
on her way –
She moved the square stone
from the white
near-dead grass.
By the lightning speed
of her black hand.

Silently, with her gaze,
she commanded the sun
to send its light
down upon everything,
even the white grass.

The sun accepted
her easy command
and came down with humility.

Days after,
she passed beggars in the street,
and tucked in her silk saree
to avoid their stains.

Seeing this,
the sun hid behind clouds,
and rain came,
unexpectedly, like tears.

Nurunnessa Choudhury

Squirrel

With a rocketing rip
Squirrel will zip
Up a tree-bole
As if down a hole.

He jars to a stop
With tingling ears.
He has two gears:
Freeze and top.

Then up again, plucky
As a jockey
Galloping a race-
Horse into space.

Ted Hughes

Out of a star which may not exist

Out of a star which may not exist,
across unthinkable spaces,
zooming through Nebulae which consist
of deadly thermonuclear mist
and veering between spheres that once
were Red Giants or Dying Suns,
a single starship races.

Condemned for ever to traverse
the Circles of the Universe
in a vast recurrent pattern
from Sirius to the rings of Saturn
and huger in its orbit than
the Ellipses of Aldebaran,
this lost ship of the Solar Seas
navigates the Galaxies.

Seated in remote control
like a god or a lost soul
goggled, helmeted and seeming
as though permanently dreaming,
voyaging through Triple Time
to the Relative Sublime
this Pilot of the Outer Spaces
conscious of the doom he faces
– Death, or a fate even worse –
bursts out of the Universe.

George Barker

Begged

He begged for a dog
with four fur paws,
with a bark and a wag
and a wet nose,
with a collar and lead and a drinking-bowl,
with a full-moon howl;
he begged, begged,
begged for a hound
with a cocked-leg and a grin and a growl,
with a basket, a blanket, a bone,
with a feeding-dish
and tricks with a ball,
a dog that would fetch and sit and heel.

He got his wish,
awoke in the black and barking dark –
the moon like a fang
in the mouth of night –
and, terrified, turned on the light:
smile of a wolf,
yeti's paws at his neck,
yard of tongue, pink, wet,
butcher's breath.
He felt like death,
he felt sick,
then he felt the first fierce frantic lick
of the dog's dog love.

A love that sobbed
if he left the room,
clawed and scratched
at the closing door,
puked on the floor,
howled and yowled fit to wake the dead
till it shared his bed –
man's best friend's head
on the pillow,
eyes rolled back in their sockets,
blind, yellow.
Good dog, good chap, good boy,
good fellow …

He longed for a good night's sleep,
a bath, a quiet meal
or a TV dinner,
an hour with a book.
He grew haggard, thinner,
but at his heel
the hound grew huge,
padded along
with the *News* in its jaws,
sat at his feet like a welcome mat
till he begged –
how he begged –
for a gerbil, a tortoise, a hamster, a rabbit,
  a goldfish, a cat.

Carol Ann Duffy

The Pearl

Inside
An oyster shell
Glows a drop of moonlight,
Polished by the stars when it fell
Through night.

Avis Harley

The Watermelon Man

Don't swallow those slippery
Watermelon seeds
Or out of your ears
You'll see that weeds
Are beginning to sprout
And without a doubt
Before you blink
Something *green* will grow out.

It will dangle from your toes
This long clinging vine
And curl around your knees
Like a thick piece of twine
Over your shoulder
Around your tummy
You'll look like a green
Egyptian mummy!

So chew as carefully
As you can
Or you could become…

Sheree Fitch

Radish

The radish is
the only dish
that isn't flat
but spherical.

Eating small
green peas off it
could make you quite
hysterical!

N M Bodecker

Owl

At four in the morning, when
darkness still clung to the trees and
in the valley, then, as a clock
shuddered, somewhere, in that dark,
afar, when an icy palace seemed to
break into jagged crystals, afar, in
the next room, in my heart, in that
dark, an owl sailed through the
night. Shrieking, it rode the billows
of the air, blent with the darkness of
the branches, then, rising, became a
stark outline against the sky. As it
came nearer and nearer its cry was
louder and louder. In a moment
when the icy lunar glitter failed to
beat, its cry passed over me, over the
roof, over the dark, into nothing,
leaving my mind a void, blank.
Unthinking, trying to think, until
five I waited. At five rain came
playing on the window and
concentrating on its sound I slept.

Brian Morse

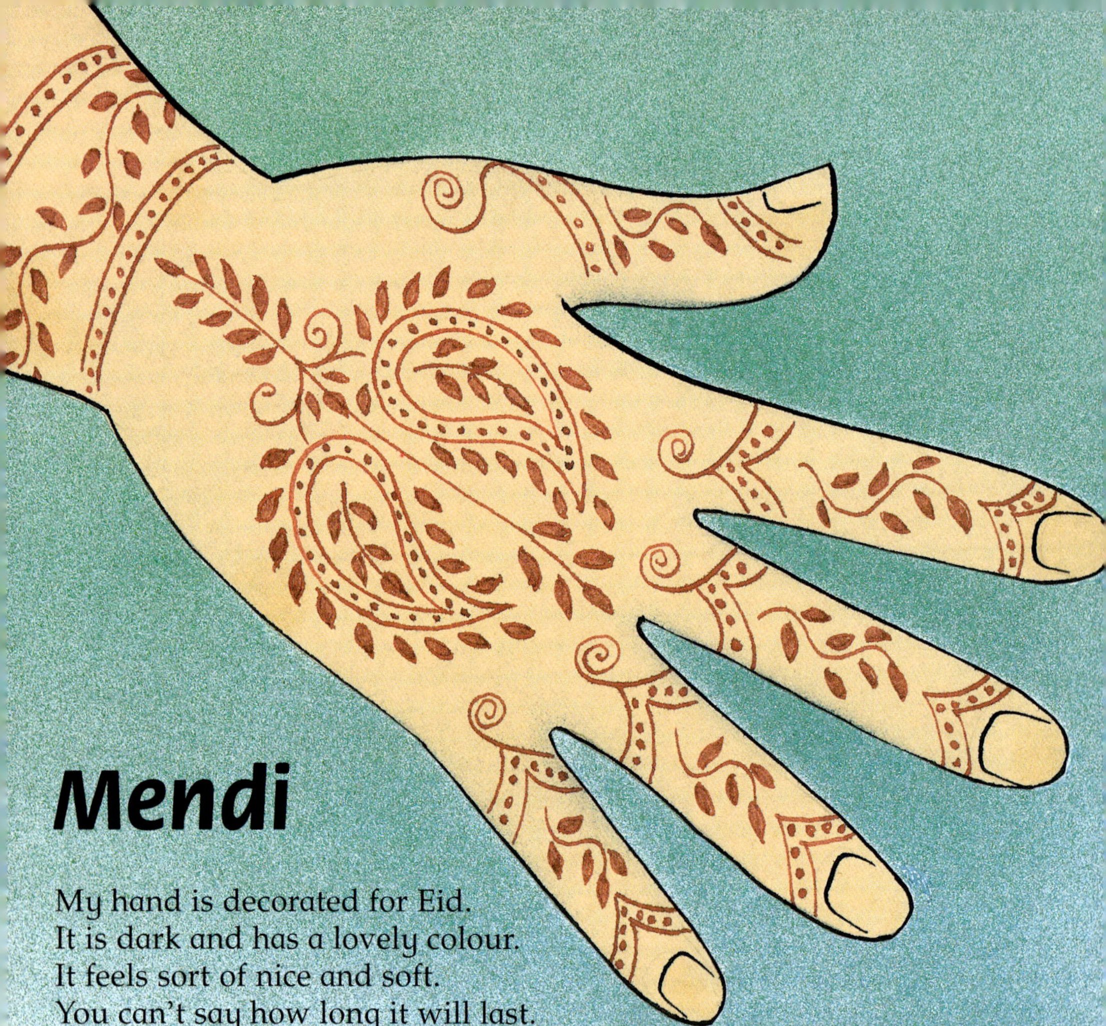

Mendi

My hand is decorated for Eid.
It is dark and has a lovely colour.
It feels sort of nice and soft.
You can't say how long it will last.
The pattern is beautiful and covers your hand.
You feel kind of special.

Mendi is made of crushed henna leaves.
It feels really nice when you put it on.
But it looks like mud with water in it
and it is a squiggly, gungy and tickly thing.

Sherin

Sidewalks

A sidewalk is a wide walk
A let's-step-out-and-stride-walk
A two-abreast-let's-glide-walk
An arm-in-arm-let's-talk-walk
A pigeon-and-a-bug-walk
A shoulder-hugging-snug-walk
A hot-dog-and-balloon-walk
An under-sun-or-moon-walk
A grass-grows-in-the-crack-walk
A rainy-day-wet-track-walk
A place where you and I walk
And talk and talk and talk.

Patricia Hubbell

Incidents in the Life of my Uncle Arly

I

O my aged Uncle Arly!
Sitting on a heap of Barley
Thro' the silent hours of night,
Close beside a leafy thicket:
On his nose there was a Cricket,
In his hat a Railway Ticket
(But his shoes were far too tight).

II

Long ago, in youth, he squander'd
All his goods away, and wander'd
To the Tiniskoop-hills afar.
There on golden sunsets blazing,
Every evening found him gazing,
Singing: 'Orb! You're quite amazing!
How I wonder what you are!'

III

Like the ancient Medes and Persians,
Always by his own exertions
He subsisted on those hills;
Whiles, by teaching children spelling,
Or at times by merely yelling,
Or at intervals by selling
'Propter's Nicodemus Pills'.

IV

Later, in his morning rambles
He perceived the moving brambles
Something square and white disclose;
'Twas a First-class Railway Ticket;
But, on stooping down to pick it
Off the ground, a pea-green Cricket
Settled on my uncle's Nose.

V

Never—never more—oh! never,
Did that Cricket leave him ever,
Dawn or evening, day or night;
Clinging as a constant treasure,
Chirping with a cheerious measure,
Wholly to my uncle's pleasure
(Though his shoes were far too tight).

VI

So for three-and-forty winters,
Till his shoes were worn to splinters,
All those hills he wander'd o'er,
Sometimes silent; sometimes yelling;
Till he came to Borley-Melling,
Near his old ancestral dwelling
(But his shoes were far too tight).

VII

On a little heap of Barley
Died my aged Uncle Arly,
And they buried him one night;
Close beside the leafy thicket;
There—his hat and Railway Ticket;
There—his ever-faithful Cricket
(But his shoes were far too tight).

Edward Lear

Of Sparrows

You never find the corpses
of sparrows the winter claims,
enough wind is around
to send those thin bones,
scrawny feathers far.
You never hear a sparrow
cry out in frozen fear,
make the slightest hunger moan;
they suffer inwardly, silently,

leaving all the groaning, the fuss,
to creatures such as you and me
behind the steamy glass,
the walled-in certainty
of our heartless houses.

Raymond Souster

Look, No Hands

Without muscles, without an arm or hand grip,
look how I wind bend back trees' big limbs.

Without wheels, without a down-hill,
look how I the sea roll and roll along.

Without a hurt, without a bruise,
look how I waterfall tumble down rocks.

Without bricks, without hammer or nails,
look how I tree build a house for birds.

Without apprenticeship, without D.I.Y. store,
look how I eagle build my family's nest.

Without getting even one single penny,
look how we apple trees give up our red apples.

Without a hose, without a sprinkler,
look how I sky water gardens with my rain.

James Berry

Kennings Cat

Tail-flicker
Fur-licker
Tree-scratcher
Mouse-catcher
Basket-sleeper
Night-creeper
Eye-blinker
Milk-drinker
Lap-sitter
Ball-hitter
Fish-eater
Fire-heater
String-muddler
Kitten-cuddler
Angry-hisser
Wet-kisser
Wall-prowler
Moon-howler
Cream-lapper
Claw-tapper
Cat-flapper

Sandy Brownjohn

One Hot Belly

One hot belly
One big ear
One round lip
With two more near.

George Szirtes

It is Snowing

It is snowing
it is snowing
and the world is white
white
white
snow falls from the sky
in small drops
in big drops
in whole showersful
sometimes it is gentle
and plays with you
it falls softly on your nose
sometimes it falls so hard
you want to cry
Sometimes it becomes a blizzard
a storm
and you cannot go to school
or out to play
you watch the storm from your window
with your nose pressed against it
When the snow settles
you can ski
skate
go tobogganing
or make a snowman or woman

In Spanish snow is la nieve
In Swahili snow is Theluji
and
In French snow is la neige
The Inuit people have 22 different names for snow

Afua Cooper

An Emerald is as Green as Grass

An emerald is as green as grass;
A ruby red as blood;
A sapphire shines as blue as heaven;
A flint lies in the mud.

A diamond is a brilliant stone,
To catch the world's desire;
An opal holds a fiery spark;
But a flint holds fire.

Christina Rossetti

Index of poem features